From The Heart
Photos and Poetry
By Selena Millman

From The Heart
Photos and Poetry
By Selena Millman

Copyright ©2008 Selena Millman
Cover by Selena Millman

ISBN: 978-0-578-00466-2

* All poems Copyright ©Selena Millman

* Poems are Copyright ©2008, Copyright ©2006, Copyright ©2004

Poems can be found at
http://poetry.com/
(Search Selena Millman)

Poems Included:

From The Heart	Get Past
Give A Voice	Are We Teaching
My Ideal Guy	It's Time
Trying To Help	One Person Can
Too Generous?	To Give
It Matters	Hold On
If I Could	We Need Tolerance
Too Old	What Can I
What Do You See	What It Takes
A Little Bit Jaded	Wish I Could
People	You're In My Heart
Day By Day	Too Much Loss
Help To Heal	Hope
Heal The Pain	Not Me
I'll Be There	Describe Myself
In My Small Way	What Inspires Me
Lean On Me	Be Grateful
My Friendship	Thankful For
Reaching Out	For Christmas, I Wish
Special To Me	True Spirit
Think About This	
Tired Of It	
Truth, Not Lies	
Can We Fix This	
Time For Children	
Heal The Children	
Listen To The Children	
Speak Up For The Children	
Listen To Me	
Who Are You	
I Am	
How To Express	
Really Care?	
People Care	
All Causes	
Imagine This	
Am I Different	
Am I	
Another Answer	

Photo Copyright ©2008 Selena Millman

From The Heart

Everything I write
Everything I say
Comes from my heart

Why say what you don't mean?
Why pretend to care?

I'm not fake or superficial
I am 100% true

I'm not bold or blunt
Generally I'm on the quiet side

But if I say I care, I care
If I say I love you, I truly do

When I say I'll be there
I will do whatever I can to be there

When I say I'll listen, I will listen
Doesn't mean I'll know what to say
But I will listen

I am a loyal friend
And I truly care about people
I truly care about animals too

SelenaMillman

Give A Voice

We need to give a voice to the voiceless
Speak out for them

For those that can't speak out
Or for those that aren't heard

Animals and children
Can't defend themselves
They need us to speak out for them

People abuse animals and children
Both are so wrong

How can anyone hurt something
Or someone so innocent

Why do we let them get away with it
We need to do something

Why do many wildlife die
Because of people's greed

What about pets
Dogs and cats

Don't let them be put to sleep
Adopt as many as you can

If you have a pet
Treat them right

Love them
Like they'll love you

What about the poor and the hungry
Many live on the street or are close to it
Can't we help them

Why does insurance care more about money
Than helping those that suffer

Why is so much about money
Money shouldn't be the priority

We're hurting when we could be helping
Can't we see that

So many suffer
Can't we do something

SelenaMillman

My Ideal Guy

My ideal guy
Hmm, let me see

He'd be kind-hearted and loving
Being open-minded is a must

He'd see and feel with his heart
Not judge with his head

A sense of humor is good
But my guy would never be cruel

My ideal guy would be supportive
He's encourage me
And I'd encourage him

Looks aren't a priority
But I'm human so it couldn't hurt

He needs to be kind
To children and animals

He'd listen without judging
The same way I'd listen to him

My guy wouldn't be perfect
But he'd be someone
I'd feel safe and loved with

SelenaMillman

Trying To Help

That's me
Wanting to help
Trying to help in any way I can

Sometimes I wish to be rich
Not for myself
More so to be able to help others

When I read a sad story
(I mean of real life)
I always want to help

I wonder what can I do
If there is a way of contact
I contact the person to reach out

A little here a little there
I give what I can
I give from the heart

I believe in helping
It's important to help others
One day, you may need help as well

SelenaMillman

Too Generous?

Is it possible to be too generous
Or to care too much

My friends tell me
What a big heart I have

They tell me not to worry
You know about them/their situation
About others I've heard of too

I can't help it
That's how I feel

My heart goes out to them
And I want to help

My friends say
Don't stretch myself too thin

Honestly I think it through as I go
But I want to help

I don't need everything I want
I do my best to get what I need

Some can't afford anything
How can I not want to help?
It's just how my heart works

SelenaMillman

It Matters

I may not be able to change the world
I know I can't help everyone

I can't end world hunger
Nor can I give everyone a home and a job

I can't cure all illness
I can't end hate, prejudice, cruelty, and abuse

These are things I cannot do
That doesn't mean I can't do something important

If you help one person, it truly matters
If everyone helped one person just imagine

Get gifts for one family
Feed one family

Have you ever had someone thank you
Calling you Santa or an angel
Know how good that feels?

Any bit you do, it matters
Any amount of help matters

We cannot change the whole world
But we can change one life

SelenaMillman

If I Could

If I could change the world
What would I do

First thing I'd do is feed everyone
I'd make sure everyone had enough to eat

Everyone would have somewhere to live
All would have nice homes

I would heal everyone
No one would be sick anymore

I would end abuse
No animal, child, or adult
Would ever be abused

I'd end hate and prejudice
Replace that with love and concern

People would learn from each other
Not judging every little difference

Money wouldn't come first, people would
Nothing would be before people's needs

If I could I'd do all these things
Since I can't I'll do what I can
To help and to spread awareness

SelenaMillman

Too Old

I say you're never too old
To watch cartoons
If you want to watch them watch them

I say you're never too old
To play with toys
Maybe it depends on the type of toy

You're never too old to think young
Be a kid at heart

Let your mind be open
And your imagination soar

Have fun
Enjoy yourself

If you're not hurting anyone
(yourself included)
How can it be wrong?

If you think I'm too old for cartoons
I think why do you care

I'm going to be me
And I'll remain young at heart
That's how I like it

SelenaMillman

What Do You See

When you look at me
What do you see

Do you see a wheelchair
Or do you see a person

Am I kind or am I cruel
Am I loving or am I hateful

Do you know anything about me
Simply by looking at me

Do I write or read
Am I rich or poor

Tell me
What do you learn by just looking

Do you know my hopes and dreams
How about my fears and pain

You need to get to know people
Before you know what they're like

To know what someone is about
Take time to get to know them

SelenaMillman

A Little Bit Jaded

I'm a little bit jaded
But not completely

I believe in miracles
But doubt I'll experience one

I believe in love at first sight
Still doubting that'll happen to me

Hope for the best
But prepare for the worst
That's how I live

Live life moment to moment
You never know what'll happen next

Bad things do happen to good people
It's sad but it's true

Don't dwell on the bad
Get through to the good

Go for your dreams
You can't get it if you don't even try

While I'm not completely jaded
I'm at least a bit jaded

SelenaMillman

People

A lot of people judge you
They judge by superficial things
Like what is different about you

They don't care if it is something you can't help
People do not want to be friends with me
Just because I am disabled
But there is much more to me than that

Everybody is different to somebody
We all have different likes and dislikes
Different dreams and goals
That's what makes us unique

We are all similar too
Everyone needs to feel loved
Everyone wants friends
All people need the same basic things

I wish people would go by personality
And tolerate differences
We are all just human beings
No more
No less

SelenaMillman

Day By Day

I take it day by day
Sometimes minute by minute
Even second by second

There are times when the pain is so bad
I feel I cannot take anymore
Not even a second more

Is it like that for you?
Ever feel like no one cares?

Sometimes it's hard to know who to trust
Do they really care?
What's their agenda?

Do your best
Go by your heart
Trust your instincts
And don't hurt anyone (yourself included)

This is how I live day to day
Moment to moment, I do my best

SelenaMillman

Help To Heal

Everyone counts
And everyone matters
No one is unimportant

Every person has the power
to change and make a change
If each person was open-minded
And helped only one person
This world would be a better place

I have a few friends who help me
and a couple that I can help
It feels good to help
To be cared about
And loved

Everyone likes and needs that feeling
And everyone has the power to give that feeling
If you want to heal
You need to love
And don't judge
Think about it!

SelenaMillman

Heal The Pain

There is so much pain
We need to heal the pain

Every person is important
Equally important

Can't we stop judging
And stop hating

Let's be there for each other
Help each other in any way we can

You'd be surprised At what a little can do
Everyone can do something

We can help in many ways
We can do anything we want

If only we start trying
Never stop trying and never stop caring

We need to work together
To heal the world
And heal everyone's pain

SelenaMillman

I'll Be There

Do you feel alone
Like no one cares

Are you angry or depressed
Worse even

I've been down
Everyone has at some time

Good News: you're not alone
I care about you

In good times and bad times
I will be here by your side

I don't guarantee great advice
But I do promise my heart is true

Even when I don't know what to say
I'll be there to listen

Cry all you need
So what if my shoulder gets wet

I'm here as your friend
And I'm a loyal friend

Here's a hug for now
And one more for later

SelenaMillman

In My Small Way

My heart is pure
My heart is true

My mind is open
I try hard not to judge

I think before I speak
Often I say nothing at all
I know words can cut deep

If I say it then I mean it
If I don't mean it, I do not say it

I never pretend to care
What sense does pretending make?

I'm a good listener
I won't interrupt

It makes me feel good when I help
Often helping is easy to do

I may never heal the whole world
But I will help as much as I can
Even if it's only in my small way

SelenaMillman

Lean On Me

We all get weak sometimes
We're only human

Consider me your friend
And I'll be true

I'll be there when others might not
I'll care with all my heart

I will listen without judging
And let you cry on my shoulder

Use my strength to get through
I'll give all I can

Even when I can't be there
I'm there in spirit

Feel my prayers
Imagine me hugging you

I can't promise to know what to say
But I do promise to care

Let this be there when I can't
To remind you you've got a friend in me

When we are far apart
You remain in my heart

SelenaMillman

My Friendship

My friend is true
It's 100% real

If I say I'm your friend then I am
I take friendship seriously

I never pretend to care
And I won't lie to you

I'd give you everything I had
If only I had a lot

I don't have money to give
But I have my friendship and love

My heart is pure
And it's full of love

When I can't physically be there
I'm there in spirit

You can tell me anything
Even when I don't know what to say, I'll listen

I'll give you whatever I can
When you need me, I'm here

SelenaMillman

Reaching Out

I'm trying to reach out to you
I don't know if you realize it or not

I do not know how you feel about me
So I'm trying to reach out
To show you how I feel

Sometimes it is hard
To express out loud
How you truly feel

And if you can't express it
You can be filled with hurt and pain

I'm trying to connect to you
Or with you

I'm making the first step
I hope you make one in return

I can't seem to express any of this out loud
So I'm writing it down for you to read

I love you
I truly do

SelenaMillman

Special To Me

You are special to me
In a way that few others are

I don't care how you're different
I am open to learn about you

I think about you day and night
You're in my thoughts and prayers

I am here for you any way I can be
I'll help in any way I can

Consider me your friend
And I will value that friendship

Your love is worth more than money
You mean the world to me

In good times and bad
I'll still care

I believe in you
I support you

I'm proud to love you
I truly care so much

Even when we're far apart
You are always in my heart

SelenaMillman

Think About This

What do people care about
What do you care about

There are so many people suffering
Too much pain in the world

Why do people judge each other
Are differences really important
I don't think so

Why do we waste time and energy
Hating each little difference

Give me a break
Figure out what's important
I have already figured it out

Love is truly important
Look past the differences

Friends are very important
Let us help each other
Be there for each other

Let's make a difference
All you need is to honestly care

SelenaMillman

Tired Of It

I'm tired of it
I really am
Why do people start rumors
Why do people believe them
Just because you hear it
Read it or see it
Does not make it true
Can't you understand
What can I say
Rumors are usually
Cruel and hurtful
No one is safe from rumors
Not one single person
Stop the rumors
And don't believe
Everything you hear

SelenaMillman

Truth, Not Lies

Support the truth
Not the lies

Spread and defend the truth
Don't repeat another lie

Don't buy tabloids
Don't even read them

Figure out the source
Then you'll know if it's lies

Don't blindly believe
Even the media deceive

Look for a credible source
Then pay attention

Ask yourself
Does the source know the person
What can they gain by lying
This may help a lot

Once we stop judging
We have a chance to understand

Think about what I said
Let's heal the world

SelenaMillman

Can We Fix This

Children hurting
Abused and neglected

Animals mistreated
Pets, wildlife, and farm animals

People hungry
Nowhere to live
Nothing to eat

So many losing jobs
Others can't find jobs

Having to decide
Between food and medicine
What's with that

Bigotry, greed, and cruelty
Can't we open our hearts and minds

All these problems these days
Can't we fix it somehow
At least some of it

SelenaMillman

Time For Children

We need to make time
For the children

This is extremely important
Children need our attention

They need our love and support
Children need to know they are loved

Children need to know
They have someone they can turn to

Everyone needs someone to talk to
Someone to lean on

Children need to understand
They are special to us

If we don't understand
How can they

SelenaMillman

Heal The Children

Do you know
How important children are

Can you see their pain
So many are hurting

I believe it is time
To heal the children

Fill their hearts with love
Ease their pain

We need to do this
We need to help and heal

SelenaMillman

Listen To The Children

If a child speaks
Do you just say oh that's nice

Do you just dismiss what they say
Or do you really listen

Sometimes children
Don't know how to express it

But they feel things
As strong as you

Children have feelings
They have wishes and dreams

Really listen to what they say
Take children seriously

SelenaMillman

Speak Up For The Children

Children are little
Too young to speak up

Children are often overlooked
And it's a shame

We say we care
Then let's show we care
Let's prove it

Stand up
And speak out for the children

Don't work around them
Include them

Don't ignore them
Do what is best for them
What's honestly best for the children

SelenaMillman

Listen To Me

Listen to me
I mean really listen

There is a difference
Between hearing and listening

I'm trying to make a point
An important point

We need to care about each other
Feel for each other
Help each other

Is this so hard
It shouldn't be

SelenaMillman

Who Are You

Who are you to judge me
To think you know me

Who are you
To tell me what to do

Do you see how I feel
Do you see what I go through

You're not better than me
And I'm not better than you

I'm not telling you what to do
So why do you do it to me

SelenaMillman

I Am

Do you know me
I mean truly know me

I'm many things
Can you see that

I am an adult
But I am a kid at heart

I'm different
But I am the same

I'm quiet
But I have a lot to say

Do you understand what I'm saying
I sure hope so

SelenaMillman

How To Express

How can I express
What's in my heart
It's easier to feel than say

I love you
That seems simple
But sometimes the feeling is more

I love you more than words can say
Words can't express the depth
I Need You

Words don't do the feeling justice
My words are too weak

SelenaMillman

Really Care?

I don't know who to trust
Who really cares

So many pretend to care
How can I tell the difference

Do you really care about me
Your words are not enough

Who can I talk to
Who will really listen
Who will help me

What should I do
I need advice

SelenaMillman

People Care

What do you think
How do you feel

It really matters to me
Every person matters

We're all important
And we are all special

Everyone has feelings
We need to remember that

Are you hurting
Are you feeling scared and alone

Reach out
People care

SelenaMillman

All Causes

It's hard to fit every last cause
It's hard to know them all

Arthritis, AIDS, Cancer, Diabetes
Child Abuse, Neglect, Adoption
Pet and Wildlife abuse, etc

They're all important
We should do whatever we can
To help as many as we can

Figure out what cause is important to you
Then do what you can to help

SelenaMillman

Imagine This

Close your eyes
And imagine this

You are sitting
On a street corner

You're sad and alone
Maybe wet and cold

You have nowhere to turn
No one to go to

You have no job
And no money

What would you do
How would you feel

SelenaMillman

Am I Different

Am I different than you
Probably, yes I am

But different how
And how much matters

What about my age
My religion or race
My hair or eye color

What I look like
Does this stuff matter

What do you think
How do you feel

There is so much
To think about

SelenaMillman

Am I

Am I in a wheelchair
Maybe I am but maybe not

Am I black or white
What religion or race am I

Am I different
Or am I the same

To be honest I'm both
And so are you

We all have differences
But we all have similarities

SelenaMillman

Another Answer

Suicide is not the answer
It is not the only way

You may be in pain
I understand it is hard to cope

There are places to go
There are people that can help

Please do not give up
And please don't give in

Pain may be all around you
But please believe me
There is another answer

SelenaMillman

Get Past ©2004

Don't always believe what you see
Or what you think you see
People lie
People deceive

Take time to understand
Ask why if you must

If we get past the hate
We can heal this world
Heal our pain

Don't we have better things to do
Than to judge anyone
Anything that is different

People are dying
Children are abused
People are cold and hungry
No place to live

Can't we work together
To help each other

And always remember Innocent Until PROVEN guilty

SelenaMillman

Are We Teaching

Innocent until proven guilty
Rumors and speculation can be proven false

What are we teaching our kids
Our nieces and nephews

Are we teaching them right from wrong
Or are we teaching them to hate and judge

Are we teaching them they can be anything
Or are we teaching them to quit when it gets tough

Are we teaching them to love and help
Or are we teaching them to destroy and hurt

What are we teaching the children of the world
We need to sit back and figure it out

SelenaMillman

It's Time

What are we teaching our children?
What message do we send out to the world?

Do we cherish what's unique?
Or do we teach to hate anything different

Do we teach tolerance?
Or are we quick to judge and hate

Do we go for our dreams?
Or do we give up too soon

When we don't notice, the children still do
They follow our lead, so let's set good examples

Innocent until proven guilty
Don't believe rumors and speculation
Anyone can be corrupt and no one is perfect

There are things more important than money
Let's love and help

It's time to teach kindness
It's time to lend a helping hand

Think before we react
We can heal this world
All its people, children, and animals

SelenaMillman

One Person Can

One person can make a difference
Do you believe me
I hope you do

One person can help to heal
We can heal the pain inside

It doesn't take much
Just be open and care

One person can listen
Just be there for others
That is not hard

One person can spread love
Everyone can love
All people can care

Let's not judge
Stop hating

One person has the power
To make a difference
We all have it inside

Please think about this
And remember it always

SelenaMillman

To Give

This is to give hope
To those that feel hopeless

This is to give love
To those that feel unloved

This is to give strength
To those that feel weak

This is to give nerve
To those that feel chicken

This is to give friendship
To those that feel they have none

Go for your dreams
You can be anything

You are loved
You are special

Never forget that
And always believe in yourself

SelenaMillman

Hold On

So many are down at times
Reach out
Someone cares

Don't let the pain beat you
You can get through the pain

To those that feel hopeless, hold on
Hang in there and don't give up

Some may have it better than you
While others have it worse than you

What you feel is important
Because you are important

I don't know your pain
But help exists somewhere
Find it

Once you get through the pain
Happiness can begin

It's your life
Do what is best for you

SelenaMillman

Hope

As long as you live, there is hope
It's not over until it actually is
This is what I believe

There is nothing wrong with hope
To hope is normal

Hope for a better day
Hope for less pain tomorrow

Hope to get through the day
Hope your wishes come true

Don't let anyone tell you not to hop
Don't let anyone take it away from you

There is so much pain
So much negativity
We need to hope

SelenaMillman

We Need Tolerance

We really need tolerance
In this world
Why do we judge each other
Why are differences important
Why do we even care
I am not perfect
And I don't claim to be
I try to be tolerant of others
And I try not to judge
Really how hard is it
To be tolerant of others
Race, religion, disabilities
None of this matters
Why should it matter

SelenaMillman

What Can I

What can I say
What can I do
How do I make you understand

You don't understand me
You don't see me for who I am

Look in my eyes
Listen to my heart

Take a moment
Just to listen and feel

I want to stop hurting
I want to love and be loved
I want to heal the world

SelenaMillman

What It Takes

What does it take
To make a difference

Mostly it takes an open mind
And a loving heart
You need to care
How hard can that be!

Hating makes everyone feel bad
Loving does the opposite
It makes you feel good

Wouldn't you rather feel good
Than bad
I know I would

Every little bit helps
I honestly believe that

SelenaMillman

Wish I Could

Words don't feel strong enough
And I can't do what I truly want to do

I can't heal your pain and make it gone
I can't heal all your suffering
How, I wish I could

I can't fund all I want to fund
I'd buy you everything you need and then some

If I could, I'd heal you
I'd heal ever ounce of pain
I'd cure whatever you needed cured

I can't do that but I can pray for you
I can be there for you which I intend to be

In your hardest times
My friendship won't end

Lean on me and I'll do whatever I can
I won't always know what to say but I'm here

To all my friends, new and ones that I've had awhile
My friendship is 100% true
It won't end unless YOU end it

SelenaMillman

You're In My Heart

When I don't know what to say
I still care and I'm still here

No one always knows what to say
But I am true to you

I Love You is how I feel
But that doesn't feel strong enough

Hearing from you brightens my day
Your words always make me smile

I feel your love and it makes me feel joy
I am so proud of you

Knowing you has given me so much
You make me feel important

I am here for you
In any way I can be

No matter how far apart we are
You are in my heart
And you always will be

SelenaMillman

Too Much Loss

I've had too much loss
In a short time lately

My aunt died last year
My uncle died this month
A beloved friend's mother died too

To some a dog may not mean much
But my dog meant the world to me

Animal or person
Love is love

My Tyler died in February of 2008
Now we have hyper Riley

I'm a bit overwhelmed with loss
No more for a long time, please
I can hope right?

SelenaMillman

Not Me

I could be blind to people in need
Not care that they have
Nothing to eat
And nowhere to sleep
Not care that the kids will get Nothing for the holidays
I could not care that animals suffer
Or that kids are mistreated everyday
I could not care

But that is Not Me
It's not who I am
It's not how my heart works
And it's not how my heart reacts
Maybe I care too much

When I see needy people
I want to give them tons of money
But I don't have tons to give

I want to help everyone
I can't but I can help some
I'll help as many as I can

SelenaMillman

Describe Myself

How would I describe myself
What words would I use

Quiet would have to be one
I'm generally quiet and shy

Caring would be another
Sometimes I feel I care too much

Creative would be a good word
I love to create things
Writing and photos are apart of me

I'm overflowing with imagination
So imagination has to be included

I would have to include pain
For the pain I feel

Help because I love to help
And at times I need help myself

There are more words
But these are a few
What words describe you

SelenaMillman

What Inspires Me

There truly is a lot of pain
In the world these days
But there is beauty and love as well

Since I got into photography
I notice the beauty in nature

The changing of the colors
The flow of the lakes and oceans

The beauty in nature
Inspires my photography

What inspires my writing
Well that be my imagination

My imagination overflows
Sometimes I can't catch up

My heart and compassion
Inspire me to want to help

Michael Jackson inspires me to love
My friends inspire me to be there

What inspires me?
Many things

SelenaMillman

Be Grateful

If you have shelter and food to eat
Be grateful because many do not

If you are in good health
Be grateful because many are not

Do you have love in your life
From family or friends
If you do be very grateful

There is so much pain in the world
Be thankful for what you have

Don't take things for granted
Be grateful for the good in your life

SelenaMillman

Thankful For

Thanksgiving is a few days away
Almost everyone has something
To be thankful for

I'm thankful for my dog, Riley
And I'm thankful for everyday
I had with my dog, Tyler

I'm thankful that I have shelter
And have enough to eat

I am thankful that my health is not worse and that I can walk

I'm thankful for my imagination
And my creativity
Both help me deal

I am thankful for my friends
Friends are very important

I'm thankful anyone that loves me
I mean that truly loves me

What are you thankful for
Think about it then share it

SelenaMillman

For Christmas, I Wish

I wish for lots of money
Money can by nice things

It can pay for things like
Food, medicine, and insurance
These aren't always easy to pay for

I wish for good health
Can you give me that?
I don't see that coming this year

I wish for joy and laughter
We all need some of that

I wish for good cheer
Lighten up a bit
Don't take everything seriously

Do I wish to give or receive?
Getting is great
But giving feels good too

Happy Holidays everyone
I hope it's full of love
Joy and laughter

SelenaMillman

True Spirit

The spirit of the holidays
Is not getting gifts
It's not decorations

These things are nice
Of course they are

But that's not what
Christmas, Hanukkah, etc is about

It is about love
It is about giving
It's about helping

Reach out to the less fortunate
Give a lending hand

Remember many can't afford even one gift
Think of them
If you can, donate a toy or gift

Remember the true spirit of the holidays
Your holiday will be twice as special

I wish you all a safe, healthy, and happy holiday season

SelenaMillman

Oh Heavenly Father

I thank you for being awake and alive
I thank you for having kept me safe this day
Please look out for and protect
The innocent
The abused
The sick
The disabled
The poor
The hungry
The helpless
The hopeless
The kidnapped
The slaves
The lost
The missing
The runaways
The orphans
The foster children
The sponsored children
And all the innocent animals in the world
Please protect the animals
From people's greed and corruption
Please look out for and protect
Everyone I care about

Amen

Photo Copyright ©2008 Selena Millman

Photo Copyright ©2008 Selena Millman

My Dogs Photos Copyright ©2008 Selena Millman

Tyler (Briard)

Born August 1992
Died February 10th, 2008 (3:00 P.M. EST)

We got him from a Humane Society in Mentor Ohio. He was just 8 weeks old then. He whimpered as we left his cage to look at another puppy. Tyler has had my heart ever since.

Riley was born in February 2006 (making him a little over 2 years old). We got him in March 2008 from the Cleveland Animal Protective League (APL). He is a Beagle mix. Mixed with what I don't know.

I am thankful for both dogs

My Lulu Storefront: http://www.lulu.com/heal4michael

My Freewebs Page: http://www.freewebs.com/heal4michael/

Need A Friend, I'm Here
http://www.care2.com/c2c/group/needafriend

PAY IT FORWARD HELP OTHERS IN NEED
http://www.care2.com/c2c/group/philanthropy

Care2 Little Angels in crises
http://www.care2.com/c2c/group/angelkids

Photographers, Writers, & Artists
http://www.care2.com/c2c/group/photographerswritersandartists

Selena's Books & Photos
http://www.care2.com/c2c/group/selena_books_photos

Small/Medium NonProfits & Charities Co-Op
http://www.care2.com/c2c/group/nonprofitsandcharities

Wish Central
http://www.care2.com/c2c/group/wishes

the Front Porch
http://www.care2.com/c2c/group/c2talk

Hope for the Holidays, A helping hand for needy families
http://www.care2.com/c2c/group/christmas

Note from Selena:

With my writing I try to inspire and reach out. I've been writing for many years. I love writing poetry but fiction will always be my first love. In my fiction, my characters are my first priority. All my writing comes from my heart.

You can find my other books at http://www.Lulu.com/heal4michael

Selena Millman
December 8, 2008

Jodi, you have been my friend longer than anyone else. Jennifer, we have been through so much together. Amanda, even though we never met face to face you are one of my best friends. I thank you all for your friendship.

I thank all my friends for their friendship. You all mean so much to me.

Uncle Norm, thanks for your encouragement.

Michael Jackson, you are my inspiration. I will always love you and your children.

www.ingramcontent.com/pod-product-compliance
Lightning Source LLC
Chambersburg PA
CBHW041538220426
43663CB00002B/69